GEORGE WASHINGTON DIDN'T HAVE WOODEN TEETH

EXPOSING MYTHS ABOUT THE FOUNDING FATHERS

BY RYAN NAGELHOUT

Gareth Stevens
PUBLISHING

Please visit our website, www.garethstevens.com. For a free color catalog of all our high-quality books, call toll free 1-800-542-2595 or fax 1-877-542-2596.

Library of Congress Cataloging-in-Publication Data

Names: Nagelhout, Ryan, author.
Title: George Washington didn't have wooden teeth : exposing myths about the founding fathers / Ryan Nagelhout.
Description: New York : Gareth Stevens Publishing, 2017. | Series: Exposed! Myths About Early American History | Includes index.
Identifiers: LCCN 2016037125| ISBN 9781482457247 (pbk. book) | ISBN 9781482457254 (6 pack) | ISBN 9781482457261 (library bound book)
Subjects: LCSH: Founding Fathers of the United States–Juvenile literature. | United States–History–Errors, inventions, etc.–Juvenile literature.
Classification: LCC E302.5 .N35 2017 | DDC 973.3092/2–dc23
LC record available at https://lccn.loc.gov/2016037125

First Edition

Published in 2017 by
Gareth Stevens Publishing
111 East 14th Street, Suite 349
New York, NY 10003

Designer: Sarah Liddell
Editor: Therese Shea

Photo credits: Cover, p. 1 (Independence Hall) DcoetzeeBot/Wikimedia Commons; cover, p. 1 (Washington) Scewing/Wikimedia Commons; cover, p. 1 (Hamilton) Hohum/Wikimedia Commons; cover, pp. 1, 15 (Franklin) Hello world/Wikimedia Commons; cover, p. 1 (Adams) Futurist110/Wikimedia Commons; background texture used throughout IS MODE/Shutterstock.com; ripped newspaper used throughout STILLFX/Shutterstock.com; photo corners used throughout Carolyn Franks/Shutterstock.com; p. 5 MarshalN20/Wikimedia Commons; p. 7 (both) Science & Society Picture Library/Contributor/SSPL/Getty Images; p. 9 Archive Photos/Stringer/Archive Photos/ Getty Images; p. 11 (Washington's tomb) Alfred Eisenstaedt/Contributor/The LIFE Picture Collection/Getty Images; p. 11 (William Thornton) Slowking4/Wikimedia Commons; p. 13 Universal History Archive/Contributor/Universal Images Group/Getty Images; p. 15 (Poor Richard's Almanac) Ando228/Wikimedia Commons; p. 17 (White House) MPI/Stringer/Archive Photos/Getty Images; p. 17 (President's House in Philadelphia) BoringHistoryGuy/ Wikimedia Commons; p. 19 Bettman/Contributor/Bettman/Getty Images; p. 21 (Thomas Paine) Louis S. Glanzman/ Contributor/National Geographic/Getty Images; p. 21 (*Common Sense*) Niki K/Wikimedia Commons; p. 23 (Jefferson) Futurist110/Wikimedia Commons; p. 23 (Adams) VladiMens/Wikimedia Commons; p. 25 (Thomas Jefferson Randolph) Nickelfan/Wikimedia Commons; p. 25 (Monticello) Martin Falbisoner/Wikimedia Commons; p. 27 (James Madison) MPI/Stringer/Archive Photos/Getty Images; p. 27 (Dolley Madison) Stock Montage/ Contributor/Archive Photos/Getty Images; p. 29 Superstock/Getty Images.

Printed in China

CPSIA compliance information: Batch #CW17GS: For further information contact Gareth Stevens, New York, New York at 1-800-542-2595.

CONTENTS

Words in the glossary appear in **bold** type the first time they are used in the text.

TO TELL THE TRUTH

The Founding Fathers were those who were key in the creation of the United States. You probably know some of them by name, such as George Washington, Thomas Jefferson, and Alexander Hamilton. There are many stories about these men who helped found America more than 240 years ago. But did you know that some of those tales aren't true?

Did George Washington really chop down a cherry tree? Did Benjamin Franklin discover electricity? Let's take a look at some common **myths** about the Founding Fathers.

Lots of weird "facts" about the Founding Fathers simply aren't true. Read on to find out what's real and what isn't!

5

THE TRUTH ABOUT GEORGE

GEORGE WASHINGTON HAD WOODEN TEETH.

THE FACTS:

Washington had problems with his teeth all his life. In letters, he said his teeth often hurt, would fall out, or had to be pulled out. He also had man-made, or false, teeth called dentures that were sometimes too big!

Those dentures, however, weren't made of wood. Dentists made them out of animal and human teeth, hippopotamus ivory, brass screws, lead, and gold wire. No one knows where and when the wooden teeth myth began, but it was even taught in schools for many years!

Philadelphia 20. Feb 1795

Sir,

Your last letter, with its accompaniment, came safe to my hands on tuesday last. —

Enclosed you will receive sixty dollars in Bank notes of the United States. — In addition to which, I pray you to accept my thanks for the ready attention which you have at all times, paid to my requests, and that you will believe me to be, with esteem, — Sir

Your very H^ble Ser^t

G. Washington

...wood.

TERRIBLE TEETH

Washington kept some of the teeth pulled out of his mouth to use them in dentures. He also bought teeth from other people!

7

THE MYTH: GEORGE WASHINGTON ONCE CHOPPED DOWN A CHERRY TREE AND COULDN'T LIE ABOUT IT.

THE FACTS:

The story goes that young Washington once chopped down a cherry tree with a small ax given to him by his father. Washington then told his father what he did, saying, "I cannot tell a lie." This tale was meant to show how honest the first US president was. But it probably isn't real!

Writer Mason Locke Weems added the story to an 1806 **biography** of Washington. The account, however, doesn't show up in earlier printings of the biography!

DAMAGED, NOT DEAD

Weems's account said that Washington harmed the cherry tree, but didn't chop it down. Washington was just 6 years old in the story.

Historians can't find any proof the cherry tree myth ever really happened, but many people have retold the story over the years.

THE MYTH: AFTER GEORGE WASHINGTON'S DEATH, SOMEONE TRIED TO BRING HIM BACK TO LIFE.

THE FACTS:

This never actually happened, but someone did want to try! In Washington's time, **medicine** wasn't an exact science. In fact, many people worried about being buried before they were dead. Washington himself asked his family and friends to wait 3 days before burying him when he died, just in case!

William Thornton was a doctor and friend of Washington's who was asked to visit in 1799. When Washington died of a throat illness before Thornton arrived, Thornton wanted to "attempt his **restoration**" with lamb's blood.

Washington died on December 14, 1799. Thornton wrote: "[Washington] died by the loss of blood & the want of air. Restore these with the heat [and] . . . there was no doubt in my mind that his restoration was possible."

MANY TALENTS

William Thornton wasn't just a doctor—he **designed** the US Capitol!

WILLIAM THORNTON

ALL ABOUT BEN

THE FACTS:

Many people think that Benjamin Franklin, another of the Founding Fathers, discovered electricity when **lightning** hit his kite during a storm. Actually, when this event happened in 1752, people already knew about electricity.

Franklin attached a key to his kite's string. He felt a charge on the key, proving that lightning was made of electricity. Franklin's kite wasn't actually struck by lightning—he would have been killed! Electricity present in the air had traveled down the string to the key.

As Benjamin Franklin flew the kite, he saw bits of the kite's string standing up. That's another way he knew electricity was present.

ELECTRIC SHOCK

A German scientist tried the same test a few months after Franklin. His kite was struck by lightning, killing him.

13

THE FACTS:

Franklin didn't say this. However, writing under the name "Poor Richard" in 1737, he said something close: "A penny saved is two pence [pennies] clear." He meant that people who save money will have money to spend later.

Many other statements said to have begun with Franklin came from other people. Another famous saying of Franklin's is: "Show me and I forget. Teach me and I remember. Involve me and I learn." However, some think this was first said by Xun Kuang, an ancient Chinese thinker!

MAN OF MANY NAMES

Franklin wrote under a number of fake names, or pseudonyms, including Richard Saunders, Silence Dogood, Anthony Afterwit, Polly Baker, Alice Addertongue, Busy Body, Martha Careful, Benevolous, and Caelia Shortface.

REAL BEN FRANKLIN SAYINGS

LOST TIME IS NEVER FOUND AGAIN.

BEWARE OF THE YOUNG DOCTOR, AND THE OLD BARBER.

GREAT HASTE MAKES GREAT WASTE.

AN OUNCE OF PREVENTION IS WORTH A POUND OF CURE.

BE NOT SICK TOO LATE, NOR WELL TOO SOON.

WHEN THE WELL'S DRY, WE KNOW THE WORTH OF WATER.

EARLY TO BED AND EARLY TO RISE, MAKES A MAN HEALTHY, WEALTHY, AND WISE.

NEVER LEAVE THAT TILL TO-MORROW WHICH YOU CAN DO TO-DAY.

One of Franklin's most famous pseudonyms is Richard Saunders, or "Poor Richard." Under this name, he wrote a guide called an almanac, which is a book full of advice and farming tips for a year.

15

WHOSE HOUSE?

THE MYTH: GEORGE WASHINGTON LIVED IN THE WHITE HOUSE.

THE FACTS:

President Washington didn't live in the White House. In fact, he wasn't even alive when the White House was completed! It took 8 years to build and first opened in 1800.

John Adams was the first president to live in the White House, moving from Philadelphia, Pennsylvania, on June 3, 1800. The building wasn't finished yet, so he had to stay somewhere else for months. When Adams finally moved in, the White House still smelled like wet paint!

THE WHITE HOUSE IN 1807

ANOTHER WHITE HOUSE

The people of Philadelphia, Pennsylvania, wanted their city to remain the nation's capital, so they built a new house for the president in the 1790s. It was never used!

PRESIDENT'S HOUSE IN PHILADELPHIA

17

RIVALS

THE MYTH: THE FOUNDING FATHERS WERE FRIENDS WHO AGREED ABOUT HOW TO RUN THE NEW COUNTRY.

THE FACTS:

Many of the Founding Fathers didn't like each other! Alexander Hamilton, for example, was considered a **rival** to Thomas Jefferson, James Madison, and Aaron Burr. Hamilton was killed in a **duel** with Aaron Burr on July 11, 1804!

Thomas Paine wrote the work *Common Sense*, which argued for American freedom from England. Paine was once great friends with George Washington. However, he later turned against Washington because he disagreed with Washington's actions as president.

MURDER AND TREASON!

Burr was vice president of the United States when he killed Hamilton in their duel. He was charged with murder, but the charge was dropped. In 1807, Burr was arrested for **treason** when he tried to start a new country!

THE MYTH:
THOMAS PAINE MADE WOMEN'S UNDERWEAR.

THE FACTS:

Paine had been trained as a stay maker. Stay makers were tailors who made corsets, which were a kind of women's underwear. But where Paine's family lived in England, stay makers made sails for ships, not corsets. Paine left home as a young man, however.

In 1776, Thomas Paine's *Common Sense* was very important in getting people to support the American Revolution (1775–1783). Many people who had respected him turned against him because of his later works. Historians think the "underwear story" was meant to hurt Paine's **reputation.**

Paine's *Common Sense* sold 120,000 copies in its first 3 months and more than 500,000 by 1783. It's believed to be the most popular writing ever sold in colonial America!

COMMON SENSE;

ADDRESSED TO THE W. Hamilton

INHABITANTS

OF

AMERICA,

On the following interesting

SUBJECTS.

I. Of the Origin and Design of Government in general, with concise Remarks on the English Constitution.

II. Of Monarchy and Hereditary Succession.

III. Thoughts on the present State of American Affairs.

IV. Of the present Ability of America, with some miscellaneous Reflections.

Man knows no Master save creating HEAVEN,
Or those whom choice and common good ordain.
THOMSON.

PHILADELPHIA;
Printed, and Sold, by R. BELL, in Third-Street.
MDCCLXXVI.

HIDDEN HISTORY?

Some who study Paine's writings think he may have worked on the Declaration of Independence, but other Founding Fathers hid his role because they disagreed with his later writings.

THE MYTH:

JOHN ADAMS AND THOMAS JEFFERSON WERE BITTER ENEMIES THEIR WHOLE LIVES.

THE FACTS:

Adams and Jefferson were good friends during the early days of the United States and often wrote each other letters. However, their different views on government got in the way of their friendship. As president, Adams gave Jefferson's enemies government positions. Jefferson beat Adams in the presidential election of 1800. They stopped writing each other.

After Jefferson's presidency, a common friend pushed the two men to return to writing each other. They became great friends again, trading letters until they died.

Jefferson and Adams died within 5 hours of each other on July 4, 1826.

THOMAS JEFFERSON

JOHN ADAMS

MONEY PROBLEMS

THOMAS JEFFERSON DIED PENNILESS.

THE FACTS:

Thomas Jefferson wasn't poor—he owned plenty of land and even slaves. He did, however, owe a lot of money.

Jefferson fell into **debt** for many reasons. He didn't make much money farming, and many were in debt to him. When those people died, he didn't get his money back. He also took on a large amount of debt when his wife's father—John Wayles—died in 1774. After Jefferson's death, his family had to sell much of his land, including his home of Monticello.

THOMAS JEFFERSON
RANDOLPH

After Jefferson died, his grandson, Thomas Jefferson Randolph, posted an ad selling Jefferson's land and Monticello (above).

STANDING SHORT?

THE MYTH: JAMES MADISON WAS VERY SHORT.

THE FACTS:

It may seem funny, but people argue about the height of James Madison, the fourth president of the United States. He's often described as "short," a "small man," and "little."

Historians think that Madison was 5 feet 6 inches (168 cm) tall. That's just 2 inches (5 cm) shorter than the average American man back then. Still, he was called "small and **delicate**." We know for sure that Madison was shorter than his wife, Dolley, who was said to be "five feet, seven inches and three quarters" (172 cm).

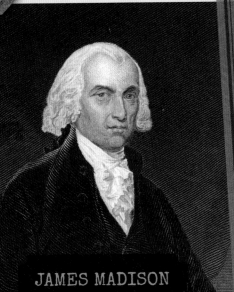

JAMES MADISON

TOWERING AMERICANS

At the time of the American Revolution, American colonists were 3 inches (7.6 cm) taller than people living in England. Scientists think Americans ate better and more food, which helped them grow taller.

Dolley Madison was described as "handsome," "tall," and "striking" by people of her time.

FIGHTING WORDS

THE MYTH: PATRICK HENRY SAID, "GIVE ME LIBERTY OR GIVE ME DEATH!" AT THE CONTINENTAL CONGRESS IN PHILADELPHIA, PENNSYLVANIA.

THE FACTS:

If Patrick Henry said this, he was at the Second Virginia Convention in Richmond on March 23, 1775. He made a speech there asking people to join him in the fight against the British by forming fighting forces called militias. His speech didn't appear in print until an 1817 book by William Wirt.

Without a recording of what's said and what happened, it's hard to know what's fact and what's myth in history. You can learn a lot trying to find the truth, though!

No one knows for sure if the "liberty or death" speech was remembered correctly. How much of it is a myth? We might never know!

PATRICK HENRY

IN THE NOTES

Wirt's account of Patrick Henry's "liberty or death" speech came from notes written by a judge named St. George Tucker who heard Henry give the speech that day.

29

GLOSSARY

biography: the story of a real person's life written by someone other than that person

Continental Congress: the governing body for the colonies at the time of the American Revolution

debt: the state of owing money

delicate: weak, sickly

design: to create the pattern or shape of something

duel: a fight between two people that includes the use of weapons and that usually happens while other people watch

lightning: the flashes of light that are produced in the sky during a storm

medicine: the science that deals with preventing, curing, and treating illnesses

myth: a story that is believed by many but is not true

reputation: the way in which people think of someone or something

restoration: the act of bringing back something (or someone) that existed before

rival: a person that tries to defeat or be more successful than another

treason: the crime of being disloyal to one's country

FOR MORE INFORMATION

BOOKS

Kirkman, Marissa. *The Life and Times of George Washington and the American Revolution.* North Mankato, MN: Capstone Press, 2017.

Kulling, Monica. *Alexander Hamilton: From Orphan to Founding Father.* New York, NY: Random House, 2017.

Thompson, Gare. *Let's Call It America! Meet Our Founding Fathers.* New York, NY: Scholastic, 2013.

WEBSITES

Benjamin Franklin
ducksters.com/biography/ben_franklin.php
Find out more about Founding Father Benjamin Franklin on this site.

Name That Founding Father
history.org/kids/games/foundingFather.cfm
Learn more about the Founding Fathers and their lives here.

INDEX